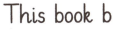
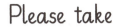

This book b

Please take

lubybuby©
WORDS AND IDEAS THAT CAN CHANGE THE WORLD

www.lubybuby.com

Published by
Lubybuby 483 Green Lanes,
London, N13 4BS, UK,
www.lubybuby.com
ISBN 978-0-9930901-2-7 Made of Love

All rights reserved.
No part of this book may be produced in any form
without written permission from the author.
Copyright© Lubna Kharusi 2014.

Made of Love

written by Lubna Kharusi
illustrated by Amir and Meliha Al-Zubi
music by Hakely Nakao Chavez, Thanae Pachiyannakis and Lubna Kharusi

Download music for Made of Love for free from www.lubybuby.com

THIS SONG BOOK IS DEDICATED TO MY DAUGHTERS AYA AND KHAIR, WHO HAVE INTRODUCED ME TO UNCONDITIONAL LOVE.

THIS LITTLE BOOK CAME ABOUT AFTER I HAD ASKED AYA WHEN SHE WAS FIVE YEARS OLD "DO YOU KNOW WHAT YOU ARE MADE OF?" ASSUMING SHE WOULD TELL ME ABOUT BONES AND MUSCLES, BUT INSTEAD SHE CONFIDENTLY ANSWERED "OF COURSE MUMMY, LOVE!"

IT WAS THEN THAT I REALIZED THAT CHILDREN INSTINCTIVELY KNOW THE TRUTH ABOUT THIS WORLD, AND YET THROUGH THE WAY WE RAISE THEM, THEY EITHER HOLD ON TO THAT TRUTH OR LOSE SIGHT OF IT.

THIS LITTLE SONG BOOK IS AN OPPORTUNITY FOR EVERYONE TO SHARE WITH YOUNG CHILDREN, THROUGH A VISUALLY STIMULATING BOOK AND A FUN SONG, THE INHERENT TRUTH ABOUT THIS WORLD, THAT EVERYTHING IN THIS UNIVERSE IS MADE OF LOVE.

WE CAN CHOOSE TO EITHER BE AWARE OF THIS LOVE, OR TURN OUR ATTENTION AWAY FROM IT. LET US TOGETHER ENCOURAGE THE NEXT GENERATION TO BE MORE AWARE OF THE INFINITE SOURCE OF LOVE WITHIN EVERYONE AND EVERYTHING, SO THAT THEY GROW TO HAVE GREATER SELF CONFIDENCE, AND ARE MORE INCLINED TO EXPRESS LOVE AND COMPASSION TOWARDS THE REST OF CREATION.

Lubna Kharusi

Flowers, birds, and trees are made of love

The earth, the sky, the sea are made of love

Laughter, songs, and we are made of love

This world is made of love.

Mommy, daddy, my family are made of love

Friends and people, we all are made of love

Food and homes, all things are made of love

Everything is made of love.

Hugs and kisses, and smiles are made of love

Today, tomorrow, all time is made of love

The sun, the moon, the stars are made of love

This universe is made of love.

Sharing, caring, and "sorry" are made of love

"Please" and "thank you", "don't worry" are made of love

Kindness, helping, and fun are made of love

All together we are love.

All hurt and fears disappear with love

Beauty, hopes, and dreams are made of love

It feels good, it feels right, then trust that it is love

Shine brightly with your love.

My body, my mind, my heart are made of love

All I do, All I say, All I am
are made of love

Let's hold hands, and pray,
that we share our love

'Cause I am made of love

And YOU are made of love

And WE ALL are made of love.